Let God Love You

Let God Love You

by

Malcolm Smith

PILLAR
BOOKS & PUBLISHING
C O M P A N Y
P. O. Box 471692
Tulsa Oklahoma 74147-1692
1-800-542-BOOK

Let God Love You
ISBN 1-880089-18-1
Copyright © 1993 by Malcolm Smith
Malcolm Smith Ministries
P. O. Box 29747
San Antonio, TX 78229-0747

Published by:
Pillar Books & Publishing Co.
P. O. Box 471692
Tulsa, Oklahoma 74147-1692
United States of America

Cover Design: DB & Associates

Editor: Elizabeth Sherman

Table of Contents

Chapter One
THE GOOD NEWS — MORE
THAN A TICKET TO HEAVEN............................1
    Human Love..6
    Divine Love 9

Chapter Two
THE MEANING OF LIFE................................13
    Choose the Real You 17
    . . . Or Be a Fake 20

Chapter Three
THE FUTILITY OF INDEPENDENCE.............23
    Lost Sheep..24
    Looking for Love in all the Wrong Places .25
    Man Redefines Life......................................28
    Man Redefines God 31

Chapter Four
IN SEARCH OF HIS SHEEP 33
    Love Without Excuses..................................35
    A Change of Mind.......................................37

Chapter Five
DAILY SURRENDER TO LOVE **39**
    Receive a Holy Hug! 42
    The Awkwardness of Truth 44
    Godly Perspective of Sin 46

Chapter Six
FREE AT LAST! **51**

Preface

It doesn't take a genius to know that many of us who are living in the last days of the twentieth century haven't a clue as to who we really are. From the materially successful business magnate to the homeless man who begs on the sidewalk, we all face the crisis of discovering our true identity and the very meaning of life.

I want to share with you in these few pages as one who, in the terror of my own lostness, found the answer; or maybe it would be better put, the answer found me. What I have to say is very simple, yet if you will think about it, it is probably the most profound truth you have ever considered.

Chapter One

THE GOOD NEWS — MORE THAN A TICKET TO HEAVEN

Three words are the complete answer to every question and inarticulate fear inside of you, and they contain the food that your inner self is crying out to be fed. Understanding these words means you will never be shackled by despair, wallow in the belief that you are worthless, or feel you are a meaningless moment in a nonsense universe.

These three life-bringing words are, "God is love." I warned you this would be simple! But please, stay with me to the end, because the revelation of these words will open a door to fulfill your destiny as a human being.

To know the love God has for you is the answer to every spiritual longing, all mental and emotional dysfunction, and in many cases, the healing of your body.

God *is* love; it is the way He *is*. This means that when you meet Him, He is love — and specifically love to you. I can say without a shadow of a doubt that God loves you. To many people this does not sound like earthshaking news. To others, it sounds ridiculous.

For example, I shared with Paula the fact that God loved her, and she turned on me with a snarl. "Don't be stupid!" she cried. "How could any God in His right mind love me? I am a worthless heap of garbage! I haven't done one thing in all my life to give me a reason to believe He could ever love me."

I could relate to where she was coming from. Many of us have said words like these at one time or another, and if we haven't said them, we have thought them. When I talk about God's love for them, most people tell me they cannot grasp what I am saying. They look over their behavior, their thoughts, words, and actions, and decide they are not worthy of such love, that it would be presumptuous to say God loved them.

Most defend themselves by saying they have done the best they could under the circumstances, which gives them reason to believe they will have earned the right to go to the "good place" after death. But they would never say that their decency earns them the right to be loved by God himself. That is something else altogether! It is one thing to get into heaven, but quite another to claim a relationship with the Creator that the word "love" conjures up.

Even sincere Christians often fall into this category. Their relationship to God is much like that of an examiner to a student. Did they pass the test of accepting Jesus as their personal savior? Did they say the "sinner's prayer"? If so, then they can sigh with relief. They will make it to heaven.

It is true that Jesus died for us and that faith reaches out to receive Him personally, but there is more to the Gospel than that.

I find many believers who have said the sinner's prayer and believe they will go to heaven, but who still wallow in a sense of worthlessness. They feel their life has no more meaning than their neighbors across the street who have no revelation of God's love to them. The Gospel is a lot more than giving the right answer to the question, "What is the basis of your being allowed into heaven?"

The Gospel, or Good News, is the announcement of the attitude of God toward us and what He has done for us because of that heart intention. God is love. He loves us! Yet, many believers wince when they hear that and say, like any pagan, "I'm not worthy! Look at the way I've lived this week."

The tragedy is that this Good News is unknown to many believers. They know only in the vaguest way that God loves them. They have read the words in the Bible and sung them from the hymnal, but the concept is totally unrelated to the real world where they live, work, and think. The love of God certainly has no miraculous effect in their lives.

So we have many believers who have the same longing to be loved and affirmed as their pagan neighbors. They live with the same anxieties over life and, in some cases, go to the same psychologist. Their only understanding of salvation is that somehow they will not go to hell if they have said the "sinner's prayer."

They have a God who only deals in the big issues, the ultimate concerns — heaven, hell, judgment, damnation, repentance, and annual pledges to the church. He is not the God of immediate concerns. He has nothing to say about the state of our mind when our stress level has gone through the roof . . . nothing to say to the empty heart who silently screams for love, who is lonely even in the presence of those who love them . . . nothing to say when we are depressed and feeling that life is no longer worth living.

However, He is not only the God of ultimate concerns. He is the God who loves us, and he communicates that love to us in the here and now — which is the secret of life itself. The secret of life is not having enough faith or finding the secret of unlimited cash flow.

Life begins when we know we are loved unconditionally by Someone. That Someone creates love in us by loving us. To such a One we respond with rest-filled faith. Such divine love gives us all the contentment we have ever searched for.

The three words, "God is love," constitute the difference between Christianity and every other religion in the world. The entire Bible is written on the foundation of these three words. Every hope we have of acceptance from God, becoming His child, being forgiven, enjoying mental and emotional wholeness, salvation now and forever, is in the three words — "God is love."

Our problem is, we do not understand the nature of His love. *We assume God's love is human love taken to the infinite degree.* This is what we thought as children, and we never updated our thinking in adulthood. We understood that husbands love wives, mothers love children, and love is love. Thus, when we say that God loves, we mean the same thing, only much more so.

However, God's love is another kind of love altogether from human love. In fact, God's love is the opposite of what the natural mind understands of the word "love."

Human Love

When we use the word "love," we are talking about a love of those things which are lovely. Love is the desire to possess the most beautiful, highest, best, most desirable, and admirable. When we speak of human beings loving, we mean that we have been arrested by another's loveliness. Their beauty of body, mind, disposition, or spirit excites us.

Someone's beauty drew the emotion of love out of us, and we wanted to possess them and be possessed by them. Our love for them was called forth by who they were, the kind of person they were, and how they pleased our eyes and mind — how they fulfilled our concept of harmony and beauty.

The universal expression, "fall in love," describes this process correctly. When we say "fall," we describe something happening to us that is essentially beyond our control. If we report that we have fallen off a cliff, we are communicating that we did not plan to do it. If we had *planned* to go over the side, we would have used the words "leaped" or "jumped."

Human love is not primarily a choice we make, but something that happens *to* us. We did not plan to love someone. We "fell" in love because of who the beloved is. They have over-whelmed us with their beauty, we are caught up in the vision of their loveliness, and we want to share our lives with them forever.

Wherever this is the definition of love, those who want to be loved by someone will make themselves appear beautiful in order to attract and be loved by that special someone. They cover and mask their faults and dress to accent their best qualities. They work hard to be the person they believe the intended lover admires, the person he or she could love. Using wile and subtlety, they try to manipulate the other to fall in love with them.

If all this effort meets with rejection, there is nothing but hopelessness and worthlessness. They have proven to themselves and everyone whom they admire and respect that, upon reach-ing for the highest, best, and most beautiful, they were found wanting. They did not make the grade.

On the other hand, if the catch has been made and life together begins, the mask will eventually come off and an equal torment will occur. With the mask gone, fear and anxiety arise, and they inwardly ask the questions: "Am I really all this person wants and needs? Am I

7

enough for them? I don't feel loved. Do they still love me? Have they seen through to how unlovely I am?"

In the knowledge that we are imperfect, human love lives with the fear that rejection is never far away.

Another expression of human love appears on the surface to be very different, but it is essentially the same. It is the love that acts on behalf of the wretched, i.e., the poor, homeless, starving, sick, and dying. In this case, the degree of the person's wretchedness calls forth love.

At the sight of children on the edge of starvation, we are moved within and are ready to give and to do. The more wretched the case, the more we are moved. The pitiable sight controls and manipulates our love.

Millions of believers transpose both aspects of this human understanding of love onto the divine. They believe God is swept off His feet by their spiritual beauty and inspiring lives of holiness. He falls in love with them as they spend their days masking themselves behind religious rituals and promises to be good. In their zeal, they hope He will be excited and aroused to love them.

Sunday church for many people is like touching up their makeup in the bathroom, hoping God will notice them and finally come to love them. Such believers live a Christian life constantly wondering whether they are still loved or whether God has seen through all their promises and walked off in disgust.

Then there are those who are poor and downtrodden. They believe their suffering is a means to please God. Somehow, they have a corner on holiness and purity because of the poverty or the sub-human treatment they are enduring. Ironically, they fear any manner of blessing or prosperity, because they would then be faced with the task of proving themselves to God on totally different terms.

When we speak of God's love, we must never think of it in terms of any type of human love; the two are not even related.

Divine Love

"God is love." He does not *have* love — He *is* love. Where human love is aroused, called forth by its object, and is open to manipulation by that object, God's love is not excited in Him by an outside influence — good or bad. He loves because that is the way He is.

God never falls in love, because He is love! His love for His creature man is not an emotion aroused by the holy beauty of our behavior or the loveliness of our morality. God does not love us because we are spiritually the most beautiful people, those with Olympic track records in righteousness! Nor is His love triggered because we are so wretched and miserable.

God loves us because of who He is, not because of who we are.

God's love can never be earned. He is not for sale! We cannot manipulate His love for us with our behavior or circumstances. His love arises from within Himself. He loved us before we were born, before we had any track record of behavior or circumstances to present to Him. His love can only be received with open-mouthed wonder and grateful thanks.

When we try to earn His love or be worthy of it, we actually push ourselves away from it. Because His love arises from who He is, it must always be a gift, always freely bestowed upon us, always unconditional.

Why does the sun shine on the lake? Is it because the lake shines like the sun? No! The sun shines on the lake because the lake is there! The lake is warm and radiant, shining like the sun because the sun first shone on it. Apart from the sun shining on it, the lake would be grey and cold.

In all that God is, He is limitless, which means His love is limitless. You could say that He loves each one of us as if we were the only ones He ever created. Each one of us has His total attention and is the object of His concern, as if there were no other humans to whom He must give His attention. We are never out of His thoughts for a second, whether we are asleep or awake, whether we succeed or fail.

God is unchangeable, and His love is as predictable as He is. He will never warm or cool in His love for us. By receiving His love, we do not run down His supply! He will never love us more than He does at this very minute, nor will He become bored with us and leave us for a new and more exciting lover! All that His love has been, He is now and ever shall be — **the same yesterday and today, yes and forever** (Hebrews 13:8).

Chapter Two

THE MEANING OF LIFE

To live in the consciousness of God's love is not an option to us. We were created to function as human beings in the knowledge that we are unconditionally loved by our Creator. In our knowing and responding to that love, we can fulfill our deepest spiritual nature and function in all our relationships with other humans. In this knowledge of His love for us, we can find the meaning to our existence and the ultimate purpose of our being alive.

Created to be loved by the Creator, we cannot function apart from that love. Separated from Him, we are lonely, spending our days searching for a substitute love that is big enough to satisfy the void within that was specifically made for the divine love.

Even when we are in close relationship with another human or humans, there is an emptiness in our deepest self that cries out for the ultimate relationship. The happily married are still conscious of a need that no human can satisfy, an ultimate relationship of which earthly marriage is but a picture. Some go through life changing mates, looking for that final and perfect lover.

What we do not realize is that the ultimate marriage is with God, and out of that union, we are able to begin to truly love other humans. Apart from living in the love God has for us, we are incapable of loving another human as we were intended to; there is the potential for death in every relationship. In His love for us, all our other relationships are made alive and have meaning.

We were created to experience this love from God. Many believers say that God loves them, but they have never understood the nature of that love, nor have they experienced that love communicated to them in their innermost being. God's love is the fuel that energizes us from within, the source of our deepest life out of which we function as persons.

It is difficult to illustrate this kind of love from our experience. The Holy Spirit directs us to one time in our lives when we approach it, but He assures us that God's love is more vast than the illustration.

"Can a woman forget her nursing child, and have no compassion on the son of her womb? Even these may forget, but I will not forget you."

Isaiah 49:15

A mother loves her children unconditionally, not because they are beautiful, cute, well-behaved, or mentally brilliant. She loves them simply because they are there. They are living, breathing, little human beings. She is there for them day and night. She sleeps, but at a whimper from one of them, she is fully awake, attending to their needs.

She bestows her unconditional love on her children with words, eyes, and hands, and they come to know themselves as unique, separate individuals who are worthy of love. The future behavior of a child depends a great deal on the love which is showered upon them as they nurse securely at the mother's breast.

Multiply the love of mother for child a trillion times and, from such a vantage point, we may look through the mist and begin to see at least the shape of God's love for us. He loves us because we exist, live, and breathe, not because we exhibit such holy behavior or so gallantly endure hardship.

When we open our whole being to His love, we find our true identity, discovering that we are not improved animals, but the friends and loved ones of God. The only foundation for respecting our fellow human on the planet is not because they please us, but because we know that they, like we, are unique creations of God, loved by Him.

In His love, we realize our significance and worth as a person. Our worth is not found in ourselves, but in the fact that God has set His love on us. The work of art finds its value not only in its beauty, but in the signature of the artist.

God's love for us, first of all, gives us worth, and then calls and coaches us to our fullest potential and beauty as the humans He planned us to be. Knowing we are God's loved ones gives meaning to our existence. We live out our days receiving His love and doing all our work in response to Him.

The result of receiving His love is complete wholeness as human beings. Moses wrote,

O satisfy us in the morning with Thy lovingkindness, that we may sing for joy and be glad all our days.
Psalm 90:14

Joy is the by-product of functioning according to our original blueprint, of having meaning and purpose in our lives. Created to live in His love, Moses describes joy as the side effect of being satisfied with His love.

This is the destiny of every man, what a person really is. Apart from our union with His love and living from Him as our source, we do not know who we really are.

Choose the Real You

From the moment of our birth, our face becomes the focus of attention. Although it will mature over the years, it is fully formed at birth and will remain essentially the same. Our face is not only our identification to loved ones and friends — the picture of my face stands on my father's dressing table, his remembrance of me — but also to the world at large. Upon entering another country, I must identify myself by the photograph of my face on my passport.

To many people, my face is who I am. But, of course, it is not who I am; it is only the face of my physical outer man. Inside my physical man is my true invisible self, which also has a face. The face of my inner man is the focused expression of who I *really* am at the heart of my being.

This true face is different from the physical shell in which it is housed. This face does not come fully formed. At birth, our inner man is without features or any specific shape. The face of our inner man will be shaped and formed by the choices we make in life. Ultimately, we will either attempt to define ourselves independently

17

of God, or to take our true place through finding ourselves in the love of our Creator.

We have no control over our physical face because it depends on genetics — the angle of our nose, the color of our eyes or skin, the set of the mouth, and the shape of the jaw have all been passed on to us from our ancestors. One cannot be responsible for the kind of face he is born with! But our inner face is formed by our responsible choices, the most significant choice being the response we make to God and His design for mankind.

Jesus said to him, "I am the way, and the truth, and the life; no one comes to the Father, but through me."

John 14:6

Jesus has just fully articulated the answer to every dilemma and torment man faces when He tells us He is the way back to the Father. Jesus brings us into intimacy with our Creator, the only One who can give us eternal life, which is meaning, purpose, and everlasting joy through knowing Him.

In the making and carrying out of our choices, the formless face takes on its eternal features. By choosing to respond to God's unconditional love and be the bearer of that love to our fellow humans, we are fulfilled, reaching our potential and actually becoming the person God intended us to be.

When we fulfill the reason for our creation, we bring praise to the Architect of our humanity and full satisfaction to our souls. We reflect His love from every facet of our being, as the facets of a diamond reflect the genius of the cutter.

While visiting some of the great cathedrals of Europe, I noticed that our guide always began the presentation by naming the architect and describing his goal in the particular design of the building. The buildings admired by all were monuments to the ability of the designer.

We were designed by God, and when we function according to the specifications of His blueprint, we declare His infinite wisdom, the genius of His love, and so, by being fully alive, give praise to Him. Only then are we fulfilling our destiny as humans.

Man was created with batteries not included! We must continually be the receiver of God's life and love, the fuel with which we function as humans. Without that relationship to God, we are dysfunctional.

But receiving that life from God is not automatic. Man is made in the image of God, and whatever else that means, it means we are unprogrammed and free. We stand unique in creation as responsible for our choices, the only creatures who must choose to live according to the Creator's blueprint or not, to be ourselves or reject God's blueprint, fashion our own, and be a fake.

Man must choose to freely respond to the love of the Creator; he must choose to be loved.

Possessing free will not only means we must choose to be who we are, but it also gives us the ability to choose to seek to be what we are not — independent of God, seeking meaning and purpose within our created self. And so, we must not only *receive* the love of God, but we must *submit* to His love as a creature totally dependent upon Him.

By choosing to submit to the divine love, you become the human you were created to be. The inner face of your true self takes on its eternal form and features, and your inner person uniquely radiates the love of God.

. . . Or Be a Fake

Satan came to the garden paradise with the original Lie, the alternate blueprint of what it means to be human. He promised man that a declaration of independence from God would bring about an evolution in which man would no longer be a dependent creature, but an independent god.

In essence, the devil enticed man to become someone he was not, to break the boundary between Creator and creature, and to attempt to walk alongside of God as His equal. The Lie excited man, opening up vast illusionary horizons that promised new possibilities to the meaning of life.

Adam chose to believe the Lie, declaring himself independent of his Creator. In doing so, he rejected God's love for him and banished himself from God's presence. From the moment he made this choice, his world began to fall apart. Mankind and all creation began to slowly disintegrate.

The love of God is the fuel and energy of man. Apart from that love there is no integration point, nothing that will hold man together.

Society, beginning with the first couple, began to crumble, for apart from the conscious knowledge that he is loved by God, man has no foundation or base from which to love another human. Separated from God's love to him, the only love man is capable of is mixed with selfishness and is toxic by nature. He has become dysfunctional as a human being.

As a person fallen from the relationship with God for which he was created, man seeks to make sense out of his existence while he builds his life on the basic belief that he is self-sufficient and has independent life in himself. He is in the ridiculous and futile pursuit of who he is not and never can be! Such a choice sends the delicate mechanism of his being into chaos. Like a machine that departs from its blueprint, he ceases to function.

Imagine a television set with personality and freedom of choice. Then imagine the television chooses to depart from its design and to seek a new existence with an alternate blueprint. It decides to be a washing machine! A television that is trying to find fulfillment as a washing machine is constantly frustrated because the meaning of its existence is in being a television. To pursue any other course is to be trapped in a dead end.

The significance of a television in a house is to fulfill its function as a television. If it seeks significance as a washing machine, it will experience waves of self-doubt and self-hate in facing the continual failure to be the machine it is not.

This parable illustrates to us what is wrong with man. The only creature who must choose to be who he is, chooses to be who he is not and never can be. In that choice, he is lost from the love of his Creator God and adrift in the sea of existence. He is on a lifelong search for meaning, significance, and a sense of worth.

Chapter Three

THE FUTILITY OF INDEPENDENCE

The word "sin" means "to miss the mark." Man is a sinner in that he has missed the goal of his existence. He is off course and moving further and further away from the meaning of his being alive.

When we say he has missed the mark, we are not thinking of him as having tried very hard to hit the bull's-eye and still, sadly, having missed. Man is not a young camper in archery class who is to be consoled because he keeps missing the target!

Man misses the mark because he has refused God's target and has set up his own. Man is not a pathetic mark-misser, but a traitor to the Creator, guilty of high treason for seeking to destroy the blueprint of the Creator and replace God with himself.

What he thinks of as normal existence is, in fact, the futile pursuit of the original fantastic illusion. He is pursuing a goal that does not exist and, therefore, can never be reached.

Lost Sheep

Jesus continually described mankind as "lost." He cited His mission as coming **to seek and to save that which is lost** (Luke 19:10). One of the best-known images that runs through both Old and New Testaments is of man being the lost sheep, pursued by the divine Shepherd (Psalm 119:176, First Peter 2:25).

When Jesus said we were lost, He was not speaking primarily of a destination beyond this life. If a man is lost forever, it is because he is first of all lost in this present existence. To be lost in the sense that Jesus used the term means to have missed the point of what it is to be a human being.

Rejecting the love of God, man is alone and separated from the Person who is the Author of his fulfilled personhood. He walks through life aware of a great emptiness within, a gnawing frustration that there is no point to life, no *why* to the *what* of his existence. Apart from being a dependent creature, receiving and revealing the love of God in his life, there is no meaning to his existence.

His inner face has not developed according to the design; it remains formless and without features. At the heart of his lostness is the cry, "Who am I? Why am I?" He is on a mission to find the face of his true self. His search takes many different roads, but all of them are destined for failure, because they all assume he can be defined apart from and independent of his Creator. At the end of every road he pursues is an ever increasing sense of futility and despair.

We cannot escape our true destiny — we were made to be unconditionally loved. That is the home from which we are lost. Our Creator placed an eternal, boundless void within us that continually aches to be unconditionally loved by Him. The reality of His love is the basis of our significance, eternal security, the meaning to our existence, and the sense of ultimate belonging. Until we turn to Jesus Christ to be miraculously joined to the Father, this void relentlessly drives us on in our never-ending search for love.

Looking for Love in All the Wrong Places

Man is lonely at a level no other creature can reach or completely satisfy. He finds himself lonely at a crowded party, lonely in marriage. He craves to be loved with an ultimate, infinite, and unconditional love. He will jump from relationship to relationship and bed to bed, looking for that elusive love he believes will fill his inner emptiness.

He defines satisfaction in terms of finding the human who will love enough, whose presence will fill every corner of his lonely life, and who will give meaning to his pointless existence. But no human can be present enough for his loneliness, and no love among creatures can substitute for the love of God he has rejected.

He searches the faces of those from whom he craves love, asking himself if he is lovable to them. Is he what they want him to be? He will wear any mask that will please them, as long as they will smile, accept, affirm, and love him.

Afraid he will be left unloved and alone, he subtly seeks to control the love that comes from others. He will give unwanted gifts of things and of his time in order to evoke appreciation and thanks and, maybe, love from those to whom he has given. He uses guilt to manipulate others into loving and caring for him.

We crave to be held by someone infinitely stronger and grander than ourselves. We long to love someone who can swallow us whole and, at the same time, introduce us to our own uniqueness and individuality. We hunger for the love that will call forth and fashion our inside face, that we may become true persons.

We want to be loved with an obsessive love, to haunt our beloved's very soul, to be ever in their thoughts, always missed and wanted. We long to be loved because we are alive, loved for who we are — but we do not know who we are! We are terrified that if anyone did know who we really are, they would not and could not love us.

We substitute the love of our fellow human creatures for the divine love for which we were made. We look for our significance, worth, and the meaning of our lives in their smile, praise, and affirmation.

Our lives are littered with lovers, friends, and significant persons who were incapable of giving the God-love. They were left by the wayside while we plunged on, pursuing the illusion that we could find divine love in a human creature.

We join clubs, societies, churches, and causes, hoping we will find the belonging and acceptance for which our inner selves long. We look to the positions we have attained in our work and the roles we play in society to provide significance and meaning to our existence. But all of them are poor substitutes for the Lover-God we were designed to relate to — the Creator who is our destiny.

Man Redefines Life

God's original blueprint for mankind was that the knowledge of our identity and sense of worth, and our subsequent behavior, were to proceed from the fact that He unconditionally loved us. But our believing and pursuing the illusion of independence have reversed this order, stating that we are loved because of who we are and how we act. Sin means we have totally missed the target and have reversed the process.

We seek and are many times driven to be loved in return for our performance.

In the original design, our inner face was to be brought to form and feature by responding to the unconditional love that embraced us. In our lostness, we take a crayon and draw features on our inner face, creating a phony self, hoping to present ourself as the kind of person others will love and respect.

To different groups and situations, we present a different face for each occasion. We try to manipulate others into loving and accepting us for the kind of person we are presenting ourselves to be.

So bizarre does this longing for love become that we will even put the crayon in the hands of someone else and let them draw our inside face.

We allow them to make us into what they think an acceptable person looks like.

We choose to be manipulated by others in the vain hope that we will find fulfillment and satisfaction in their acceptance. Thus, our inner face becomes covered with graffiti! We draw a face for home, another for the office, and yet another for the church.

The face that was created to be called forth to its individuality by the love of God, and to be the radiator of His love-image through that uniqueness, is now misshapen. It is filled with the reflection of other people's ideas of what it should be, copies of others, with the imprints of their fingerprints and demands all over it. And the face of the true self remains formless, the potential features that only the love of God can produce lying undiscovered.

Bearing the pain of feeling unlovable, unwanted, rejected by other humans, with no place to turn for the love that alone gives meaning to life, man takes yet another step downward. He turns from the creature to the created, to the stuff of creation: drugs, chemicals, alcohol, food, sex, clothes, endless empty hours in front of a television.

In desperation, he tries to find his meaning in a fictitious character in a soap opera or movie, or capture some thrill for his boring life in the success of a nameless character in a game show. He has announced that there is no meaning to life, no one to affirm his worth and love him for who he is. Consequently, he steps off the planet into the oblivion of the drug of his choice.

Multitudes of people exist for a lifetime in this despicable condition. They die without ever becoming real and whole persons. They become used to this state of inner death, believing it is the best they can hope for. They stagger through life ghosts of true humanness and think that is normal!

While pastoring in New York, I often took some of the young men of the church with me and ministered in Pennsylvania. In the crystal clean air of the mountains and the deep stillness of the night, they'd become restless and uneasy. They complained that something was wrong. It was too quiet and the air smelled strange!

They thought the continual scream of traffic and angry people was normal. So totally had they adjusted to pollution-laden air, they feared breathing air which was not thick with chemicals might poison them!

Mankind has adjusted to the quiet hell of separation from God's love and does not realize that what he thinks of as normal is really the night of the walking dead. Jesus came to bring resurrection to those who were dead inside, to give them a new mode of existence. The life we receive from Him is the life for which we were originally made — the design which is the destiny of every human.

Man Redefines God

As soon as man rejects the truth that God loves him with an infinite and unconditional love, he has created a terrifying monster for his deity. A God who knows all things about us, has all power and infinite wisdom to achieve His plans — but Who only loves us conditional upon our being good enough to deserve it — is the ultimate object of fear.

Man cowers before the image of God he has created, afraid because he knows he does not deserve love. He has created a God in his own image, one who loves conditionally. *If* we meet the standards of beauty and performance, then we are worthy of being loved. Out of this awful distortion of God's character, religion was born, with all the rules of behavior that would produce a life good enough to deserve His love.

Inevitably failing to keep the rules, man grovels before the terror he calls God. He makes promises that, "Given another chance. . . . " But he returns, begging forgiveness for having broken his promise one more time, for doing the very reverse of what he set out to do.

Man believes the Lie that he can, independently of God, please Him. With enough effort and dedication, he will produce a life that will gain God's love, approval, and attention.

The elusive satisfaction he seeks is the sense of fulfillment he would receive if only he could love God enough, a goal he can never attain. All his promises and dedications lead only to despair. Man is fleeing from a monstrous idol god — even while he says he desires Him!

Why do so many people who intensely follow religious rules end up in sexual sin? Because they are hungry for an ultimate love that their religion is not only failing to satisfy but, by its deadness, is stoking into a furnace of longing.

The rules of religion never satisfy! Man was not created to keep a list of rules for a Judge and Lawgiver, but to be held in the embrace of the Infinite Lover and, in the energy of that love, respond with obedient faith and love.

Chapter Four

IN SEARCH OF HIS SHEEP

Even though man rejected God and fled from the distorted idol god with whom he replaced Him, God did not reject man. God pursued him, for His love for man is not based on what man did or did not do, but on who He is — and He is love.

> In this is love, *not that we loved God,* but that He loved us and sent His Son to be the propitiation for our sins.
>
> **First John 4:10**

> And you were dead in your trespasses and sins.

> But God, being rich in mercy, because of His great love with which He loved us,

**even when we were dead in our
transgressions, made us alive together with
Christ (by grace you have been saved).**
Ephesians 2:1,4,5

The love of God is not an idea or a mystical
spiritual thought that calls out the best in us.
The love of God is action, revealed and defined
in the coming of the Son of God into the world
to take our place in death. It is the figure on the
cross Who was buried, Who rose from the dead
and was seated as Man in the heavens.

*Jesus Christ is the dictionary of heaven,
defining and giving the revelation of God's love
to us.*

We have seen that man is lost from the love
of God, like a sheep in a terrible wilderness.
Jesus describes Himself as God, the Shepherd,
who comes into the lostness of the sheep,
without Himself becoming lost, to find the sheep
and carry it to the home for which it was made.

Jesus says that each of us is uniquely *His*
sheep:

I have found my sheep which was lost!
Luke 15:6

When He says the sheep is His lost sheep,
He means that, out of all the sheep in existence,
this particular sheep is uniquely His. This sheep
means something to Him; it has a value which

has nothing to do with its being a sheep, but in its being *His* sheep in particular. He is saying that it is His sheep and, therefore, He has the right of ownership.

Also, by saying the sheep is lost, He is saying that the sheep has lost something in the separation. When we are lost from our rightful Owner, we are in a world of isolation and abandonment, desperate to find that place of love and security.

Love Without Excuses

The Shepherd comes to the sheep in non-judgmental love, not to condemn, but to save us. However, nonjudgmental love does not mean He will now excuse, cover, and lie for us like an emotionally sick mother would. Nor does He say there is something wrong with our genes, or that we are ill and cannot be held responsible for our actions.

The sheep is not left to wander aimlessly in the lifestyle of its choice. The Shepherd does not leave the sheep to its own ignorance, philosophically declaring, "Whatever a sheep wants is okay, as long as it is meaningful to the sheep."

God's nonjudgmental love does not mean He has thrown away truth and we now live in a fuzzy world where everyone is right by default. He comes for the *lost* sheep, meaning something is terribly *wrong*.

There is a place of safety, a home where the sheep is meant to be, and a way of life that brings a peace that passes all understanding. What is wrong is that the sheep is far from all these things.

Why does God the Shepherd come to live among us? It is because man is wrong and will be forever wrong apart from the intervention of the God who made him and Who alone can save him. The fact that entering into our lostness caused Him to die shows the infinite extent of our wrongness.

In another context, Jesus said He had come for those who are sick. He strongly points out that if no one is sick, there is no point in the divine Doctor making house calls (Luke 5:31)! Nonjudgmental love means the Shepherd comes not to kill the sick, rebellious sheep, but to save and heal the sheep through a relationship with Himself, where sheep are made whole.

Jesus, the love of God in flesh, confronts us with unconditional and nonjudgmental love. He does not sweep our sin under the rug, but, as no one else ever has, He brings it out and confronts us with the fact that we are severed from Him who is our life. As such, we are dead, lost, and losers. Then He announces to us that through His coming, His death and resurrection, He will personally bring us to life.

· Our response is confusion: "I don't deserve this! What do I have to do for you to save me?" And He says, "Nothing! Just admit that you need saving! I will do the saving; you are the one who does the receiving."

A Change of Mind

Jesus is the Word, the outspeaking of God. He is the divine, unconditional love of God in our flesh, our humanness. When He died, He was totally identified with our sin, shamed with our shame, and punished for our rebellion. He rose from the dead because He had achieved His end. The Law was satisfied, and man's debt for sin had been paid on the cross.

Because of His selfless act, we are pardoned. We can now experience the embrace of God's love and be welcomed into His family. The marriage of man and Creator that had always been the reason behind creation can now be a reality.

The Good News is that you and I are loved, pardoned, and welcomed to the family of God. There is nothing to do, now or ever, for all was done by the God who loves both of us unconditionally. You must now receive the love and all His love has accomplished.

God, by definition, is complete in Himself. Yet, He chose to create us and leave Himself with something he did not have — our free

37

LET GOD LOVE YOU

response to His love, our free choice to receive the pardon and enter into the divine love affair.

Repentance is an archaic word that simply means "a change of mind." Faith is the abandoning of all hope of finding meaning to life within ourselves and our efforts, and resting totally in God and His love for us in Jesus Christ.

When we respond to the message of God's love, it is always with a radical change of mind and a total resting in who He is.

When we hear the Good News of His unconditional, infinite, and nonjudgmental love, we have a change of mind that sends shock waves to the outermost reaches of our lives. We realize He is not the monster we secretly thought Him to be, but the strong Lover we have been looking for all of our lives.

We change our minds about ourselves, admitting that our whole lives are wrong because we have believed the Lie and ordered our lives by it. With an entirely new mind-set, we turn in faith to our Creator, Lover, and Savior, and we receive His free gift of salvation.

We change our minds about the very meaning of life. Upon surrendering to His love, it becomes joyously clear that the reason we are here is to be loved by God, to be filled — dwelt in — by His Spirit, and to be the demonstrators of His love in our lives.

Chapter Five

DAILY SURRENDER TO LOVE

Many believers stop at the point of salvation. To them, the love of God is a cold precept of theology which they have believed. They sing, testify, and preach about that love, but it is something "out there," separate from their inner struggles. The love of God to them is seen in Jesus dying for them *two thousand years ago* so they could choose to go to heaven when they die *in the future*. The overall and far-reaching result is that their *present* Christianity is dead and sterile in its correctness.

Millions of believers understand the Gospel as having sins pardoned and going to heaven after death. They have missed the whole point of being *found,* and so, handle the present moment with a new box of crayons!

They now use religious work, ministry, and performance of religious rituals to gain the smile and approval of men and God in their continued struggle to find love. They are found, but they never know who they are in their relationship to God in Christ. They never become persons. Their faces never take form because they will not receive the love of God *now.* They spend their lives trying to earn what they have already been given.

The understanding of God's love in the early Church was the invasion of God himself into believers' lives, making them alive as they had never dreamed possible. Receiving God's love was seen as a marriage between their inner selves and God. They became whole mentally, emotionally, and spiritually. They began to function in life. In many cases, the experience of God's love physically healed them.

The great difference between those early Christians and many believers today is that the early Christians did not meet the love of God only in the cross, but in the resurrection and the ever-present Holy Spirit. The One who died because He loved us now lives and wills to come into our lives, to actually communicate that love to us in every challenging situation.

The Holy Spirit is God on earth today, living with us in this dimension of time and space. He is the perfect revealer and communicator of the

Lord Jesus to us. It is He who opens our minds to grasp the incredible Good News that God does love us, Who actually brings us to know the love of God in our experience.

The love of God has been poured out within our hearts through the Holy Spirit who was given to us.

Romans 5:5

According to well-established tradition, at the end of the meetings of the early Church, believers would open themselves personally and corporately to the Holy Spirit. The prayer they used is alluded to in First Corinthians 16:22, where the Aramaic word is retained. They cried, *"Maranatha,"* which means in English, "Come, Lord, come!"

Maranatha is not a cry for the Second Coming of Jesus, but to the Holy Spirit, the One Jesus sent to comfort, teach, and lead the Church (John 15:26). The Holy Spirit would bear witness of Him, give believers peace in difficult situations, reveal His plan and purpose for their lives, anoint their faith with supernatural power, and fill their hearts with divine love.

We do not merely meditate and think about a Jesus who died for us two thousand years ago. We recognize that He is alive and now with us in the Holy Spirit, and we open our hearts to Him daily, allowing Him to make all that love has accomplished a reality in our everday experience.

Receive a Holy Hug!

There is a phrase used of the Holy Spirit in the New Testament that speaks directly to this personal communication of God's love to us.

While Peter was still speaking these words, the Holy Spirit fell upon all those who were listening to the message.

Acts 10:44

A more literal translation of the Greek word for the phrase, "fell upon," means "to hug" — even "to give a bear hug." The same word is used to describe the father of the prodigal son, who ran to meet his wayward son and **fell on his neck, and kissed him** (Luke 15:20 **KJV**).

A woman we will call Jill came to one of our seminars an emotional wreck. She had a history of being sexually abused as a child, and had been through two marriages where alcoholic husbands had physically and mentally abused her. During the seminar, she had seen the love God had for her and began to forgive all who had abused her.

At the close of the meeting, she came with hundreds of others for prayer and the laying on of hands. As I touched her, I became aware that the Holy Spirit was making everything I had said in the seminar a reality in her life. That night was the beginning of a journey into wholeness and the life God created her to live and enjoy.

She wrote to me later and, not knowing the biblical phrase describing what the Holy Spirit does, she said, "That night, at the end of the seminar, I came forward, knowing by faith in the Scripture that God loved me. As you laid your hands on me, the Holy Spirit hugged me and hugged me until I was alive.

"In that hug, He let me know that I was His loved one. He gave me worth and a new meaning to life. He went back to all the garbage of the past and began a great work of healing. I am still living in the energy of that hug, and knowing Him, the Person who is the life of my life, better every day."

Paul never ceased praying that he and those for whom he was responsible would mentally grasp and personally experience this healing love of God.

so that Christ may dwell in your hearts through faith; and that you, being rooted and grounded in love,

may be able to comprehend [i.e., mentally grasp] **with all the saints what is the breadth and length and height and depth,**

and to know [i.e., in personal experience] **the love of Christ which surpasses knowledge, that you may be filled up to all the fulness of God.**

Ephesians 3:17-19

Paul is praying they will have an ongoing experience of God's love in a twofold way. First, that they may have a mind continually renewed to see all of life in the light of God's love. And secondly, they may have an ongoing experience of Christ loving them by the Spirit.

We can never rest in a *single* experience of being blessed with insight from the Spirit. *Each day* we must present ourselves to Him in order for Him to teach us to understand His love for us more and more, and to experience Him loving us in the unfolding situations each day holds.

This requires a daily readjustment of our focus. We have spent a lifetime looking at ourselves as those who must do, perform, and be on our best behavior in order to be loved. We now must align our thinking with Truth and walk into each day knowing we are loved by God because of who He is, not because of who we are.

The Awkwardness of Truth

When I came to the United States from England, I spent six hair-raising months learning to drive on what, to an Englishman, was the "wrong" side of the road. I had changed countries and needed to lay down new tracks in my mind to adjust to the new truth that in America, people drive on the right instead of the left!

In the same manner, you need to be prepared to feel awkward as you begin to apply the truth of God's love. Our approach to Him and our understanding of our relationships with others will radically change. Consequently, they will feel awkward, even wrong, at first.

We have been accustomed to the burden of God being on our shoulders. To be a Christian meant to be dedicated enough, pray enough, and read the Scripture enough to attract His attention and receive His approval. We are used to the low-grade anxiety of wondering if we are loving Him enough. Are we being successful in our pursuit of Him, or are we merely fooling ourselves?

But now, we are learning that He was seeking us before we ever thought of Him! He loved us before we were born; therefore, His love for us could not be based on what we did yesterday, or will do today or tomorrow! He has pardoned our sins of yesterday, today, and all those not yet committed!

We are the object of His delight and care while we sleep; we waken to His delight in us. All of our seeking, serving, praying, investigation of truth, love to Him and other humans, is a response to His prior love for us, His first seeking of us.

This is a completely different way of life than that to which we have been accustomed. Therefore, it will take some time to learn about and feel comfortable living every day in the light of God's unconditional, all-powerful love.

Godly Perspective of Sin

When you begin to actually live according to those three dynamic and life-changing words, "God is love," be ready for believers who have limped through their Christian life along with you to be alarmed at your new attitude toward God.

Their first concern will be, "But what about how we behave? Doesn't that matter to God at all? Saying that God loves us apart from what we do is giving license to sin!"

I always smile when they accuse me of that and remind them that they were successfully racking up a lot of failure and sin before I allegedly gave them a license! The truth is, when we live our lives from and unto such love as Christ Jesus demonstrated, our attitude toward sin takes on a whole new meaning.

To begin with, we are no longer breaking a law and standing before a Judge, for all our breaking of the Law has been dealt with in the blood of Jesus Christ. Because of the cross and resurrection, we have a totally new attitude toward sin.

When we sin, we know immediately inside of us that we are grieving the One who loves us and lives in us by His Spirit. It is one thing to break a law; it is quite another to grieve the One who loves us! He means more to us than life itself, and the last thing we ever want to do is displease Him.

Receiving God's love is the key to fulfilling our destiny as humans. The command that sums up our destiny in the Old Testament is to love God and love our neighbor as ourself. (See Matthew 22:36-40). In the New Testament, Jesus summed up all of His teaching in the command to love one another with the same love with which He loved us. (See John 13:34,35).

Plainly, our purpose on earth is to love God and one another. But how do we do this? The key is in knowing and receiving His love for us.

We love, because He first loved us.
First John 4:19

We cannot and do not love others in our own strength, but in our receiving His love for us and in His coming to live inside of us by His

47

Spirit. We are filled to the bursting point with a divine love that desires only to love others.

Living in the knowledge that we are uncon-ditionally loved by God means that sick habits, formed in despair as we searched fruitlessly for love in the faces of other humans, will drop away. Instead of craving another person's love and attention, we will be showering them with the love of God that is on the inside of us.

Love has many attributes which, when put together, form the very life of the Lord Jesus. With Christ himself in the center of our being, we live from Him as the source and reveal His love in behavior. In so doing, we fulfill the Law.

Living in His love is not a license to sin but freedom to fulfill our destiny.

But what happens when we do sin? Resting in His love introduces us to a totally new way of handling our failures. In the old religious way of trying to please God and be good enough for His love, we heaped failure on top of failure by being afraid of Him, fleeing from Him when we sinned.

Like the first couple in Eden, we ran to hide in the trees at the footsteps of God. Hiding from Him and cringing in fear are clear indications that we do not believe He loves us, but is coming to reject, hurt, and punish us because we are not worthy of Him.

To illustrate how ridiculous this is, running from God when we sin can be likened to a little baby rejecting his mother's love and attention because he is not being a perfectly mature baby! Our eyes have been on our behavior instead of on Him. We have been thinking after the flesh — God will love us when we are good enough.

Knowing He loves us in our failure, even as He did in our moments of spiritual ecstacy, we can bring our failure into the light, own it, and even as we do so, rejoice that the blood of Jesus has cleansed us from all sin. "God is love" makes us free to face failure without fear, to face the music and then dance with joy!

We do not come making promises to try harder and call on willpower to be more holy. We receive with thanks the ever present cleansing (First John 1:9) and rest in the strength of His life within, knowing our own weakness a little better and thus being better equipped to rest in Him every second of the day.

Chapter Six

FREE AT LAST!

Knowing God's love communicated to us, we no longer look to the faces of others for approval or seek their love to fill the emptiness and loneliness of our soul. We know He is the love we have looked for all our lives and the presence that alone can satisfy and fill us at all times.

We can now discard our masks and drop pretenses we used to manipulate others into loving us. We do not live our lives around their approval, for we know we have His!

No longer do we go through life with a sigh because we have allowed others to set our agenda, to decide how we are to think and enjoy life. We do not live in fear that they will reject us if we do not do things their way, for we know we have His approval and are the absolute delight of His eyes.

We now learn to relate to people on the basis of what we have to give to them. If they communicate love to us, that is a bonus. We look at people through new eyes, eyes that have seen His love for every person. We know they are loved as we are!

Living in the knowledge of God's love, it becomes apparent that the sadness, crabbiness, and meanness of other people's lives arise from their broken hearts, because they are ignorant of or have rejected God's love. They do not know they are loved. But we know they are, and we treat them as such. We are able to love them, for we know we are loved! We actually become God's love to them.

Realizing the Shepherd's love in the cross and resurrection of the Lord Jesus, and the response that receives Him, is the beginning of personhood. In this turning toward the love of God, our true self is resurrected. Then our misshapen face knows His healing touch. The old graffiti of our sin begins to fall away as the true form and features of our unique self begins to emerge at the call of love.

We are resurrected the moment we are joined to the Lord Jesus. However, dropping away the old, phony faces and seeing our true self emerge takes time. The crisis of knowing we are found and loved is followed by the process of responding to that love with faith choices in every situation of life, every minute of every day.

This is the secret to obtain true joy. Joy is the hum of a life that is functioning according to the blueprint, a life that is fulfilling its destiny. As a machine has a certain hum which tells the mechanic it is functioning at peak performance, so the person who is in Christ and is always aware that Christ is in him has the hum of joy in his life.

Living in the love of God through Jesus Christ is the life of a whole, functional person. You rise each day knowing the meaning of your life and joyfully go about your business with purpose. And your complete reliance upon the One who supernaturally fills the limitless, eternal cavity in the center of your being makes every day a miracle!